Money Matters
Bible keys to true financial freedom...

by
Dan Vis

Copyright © 2023 by Dan Vis
All rights reserved
including the right of reproduction
in whole or in part in any form.

All Scripture quotations are from the
King James Version of the Bible
Emphasis supplied unless otherwise indicated.

ISBN: 978-1-958155-10-3

Published by FAST Missions
111 2nd Street
Kathryn, ND 58049

Additional copies of this book are available by visiting us at WWW.FAST.ST

Dedication

This book is dedicated to Kevin and Denise, who threw a lifeline to a desperate young man drowning in debt, helping to open a door to lifelong ministry. Your sacrificial gift will never be forgotten.

Table of Contents

Chapter 1:   Introducing Money 1

Chapter 2:   Foundational Principles 5

Chapter 3:   Get a Grip.. 10

Chapter 4:   The Dangers of Debt 16

Chapter 5:   Treasure in the House 24

Chapter 6:   With All Thy Might 31

Chapter 7:   Heaven's Mathematics 38

Chapter 8:   The Love of Money 44

Money Matters
Preface

    I wasn't raised in a wealthy family, and I can't really remember my parents ever explaining to me how money works. And before long I found myself struggling with financial pressures, tangled up in ever increasing debt.

    When I became a Christian, I made concerted efforts to change my situation--but nothing quite seem to work. The harder I tried, the worse things got. Until things were finally so bad I could see absolutely no way forward.

    I decided to counsel with a friend, and ask his advice about filing for bankruptcy. It wasn't something I felt right about doing--but I just didn't see any other option.

    My friend however, stunned me with the greatest act of generosity I've ever experienced. He pulled out his checkbook and began writing checks to pay off every one of my debts.

    I'm still stunned by what he did.

    But it gave me a whole new lease on life--and were it not for that gift I don't believe I would have been able to live the life of ministry I've enjoyed ever since. His gift changed everything.

    Money matters.

    In the years since, I've dug deep into the Scriptures to understand the secrets to real financial freedom. And while I may not be wealthy, I wake up every morning completely free to serve God in whatever capacity He chooses. My home is completely paid for. I don't have car payments or credit card debt. And I have emergency reserves in the bank. I've gone from abject bondage back then to a life of sweet liberty today.

If you are eager to experience the kind of financial freedom only God can give, the pages ahead will help...

Introducing Money
Chapter 1

Money. It's a huge part of our lives these days, isn't it?

I don't know all that much about the early history of it—and I certainly don't know who invented it. But I do know that in our day, most people seem entirely preoccupied with accumulating more and more of it. And society seems intent on swishing it around faster and faster, every day. It's a curious thing to watch.

Of course, there's a reason everyone is seeking it. As Solomon pointed out in the book of Ecclesiastes, "money answereth all things" (Ecclesiastes 10:19). Or as the NASB version translates it: "money is the answer to everything". Which is quite a statement isn't it? Money may not be able to buy happiness, but it can sure get us a lot of things that contribute to happiness!

Imagine for a moment, that someone gave you a gift of one million dollars, you could use any way you wanted. How might that make a difference in your life? Well, that's the power of money...

Or to put it differently, money matters.

The Will of God
I believe the Bible teaches that God wants to prosper us. In Deuteronomy 28, Moses promised that God would send a whole string of blessings to those who would "observe and ... do all his commandments, which I command thee this day" (Deuteronomy 28:1). They would be blessed in the city, and blessed in the field. Their gardens would be blessed, and their flocks would be blessed. Their baskets would be full, and their storehouses too. "The Lord shall open unto thee his good treasure" (Deuteronomy 28:12). In fact, Moses described it like this: "All these blessings shall come on thee, and overtake thee" (Deuteronomy 28:2). I kind of get the impression these blessings would be so great we couldn't get away from them if we tried. Even if we were to run the opposite direction, they would still come crashing down on us!

There are conditions to all this, of course, but it certainly seems God's desire is to bless.

The Worth of Wisdom
The book of Proverbs describes prosperity as the natural result of following God's principles. "Happy is the man that findeth wisdom" we read in Proverbs 3:13. Why? Because it's more valuable than "silver" or "fine gold" (vs 14). More precious than "rubies" (vs 15). And then this: "Length of days is in her right hand, and in her left hand riches and honor" (Proverbs 3:16).

We've often heard that the health principles of the Bible (leading to "length of days") is the right arm of the Gospel—and that last verse makes that point explicitly. But it also clearly suggests there's a left arm as well: money management according to the Bible, which brings financial success ("riches and honor").

I believe both arms are important today. In John's final epistle, he made it clear financial success was one of his biggest prayers for the believers in his day. "Beloved, I wish above all things that thou mayest (1) prosper and (2) be in health, even as thy soul prospereth" (III John 1:2). There are those two arms again, wealth and health. John longed for every believer to have both in their life. And so does God...

In the coming days, we are going to explore key aspects of God's plan for money management. And we'll learn how to avoid some of the pitfall's in the world's approach. Follow right principles, and you can count on God's blessing. His promises are sure!

My background is not in finance, and I'm not giving investment advice. But I am a Bible student, and I am convinced the Bible gives us everything we need to know to experience true financial freedom. Aren't you?

We'll start digging into our first key tomorrow...

Introducing Money
Study Questions

How important is money in the life of a believer? How many areas of life can it help with?

How does God promise to bless those who follow His commandments diligently?

What two blessings especially are promised to those who live by God's wisdom?

Additional Notes:

Foundational Principles
Chapter 2

In yesterday's reading we learned that God's plan is to bless us financially. That if we will commit to following His plan for money, He'll chase us down with so many blessings we won't be able to outrun them. That prosperity (and health) are the natural result of living by divine wisdom.

In the coming days, we are going to explore some of that wisdom. And specifically, we are going to look at biblical principles related to how believers should manage their finances.

What is Money?

Money in and of itself, isn't really all that valuable. You could melt down the metal in a coin and use that to make something I suppose. Paper currency is worth even less. About the only thing it is good for is kindling a fire or jotting down a short note you might otherwise forget. Clearly, the value of money isn't in its intrinsic worth.

No, money's value is that it is a medium of exchange. We measure the value of an object by its cost. And if it is valuable enough to us, and we have the money on hand, we can exchange our money for that desired item. That seller can then use that same money and exchange it for some item of value to him. Round and round it goes, with items or services changing hands, with every transaction.

This is what makes money so important. Money is not evil or good innately, it is just a means to some end. What matters then is how we use it. Which leads to our first money management key: believers should familiarize themselves with God's plan for money, and use their resources to accomplish His purposes.

A Threefold Cord

In my study of the Bible I've noticed God seems to have three primary purposes for money. This list may not be exhaustive, but in my experience, most situations generally fall into one of these categories. Here they are:

1) To meet our personal needs.

In the Sermon on the Mount, Jesus made it clear that God takes our needs seriously. "Take no thought, saying, What shall we eat? or, What shall we drink? or, Wherewithal shall we be clothed? ... For your heavenly Father knoweth that ye have need of all these things ... and all these things shall be added unto you" (Matthew 6:31-33). What constitutes a need versus a want may be a matter of some debate, and again, there are conditions to this promise. But the point is clear—if there is something you truly need, God wants to make sure you have it.

Paul made the same point in his letter to the Philippians. "But my God shall supply all your need according to his riches in glory by Christ Jesus" (Philippians 4:19). Don't you love that promise? I know I've claimed it many times over the years. And looking back, I can see clearly that somehow God has indeed always come through for me.

So one reason God gives us money is to help ensure our basic needs are met. He may use other means to supply those needs, but money (income) is usually a big part of that provision. And if God is leading in our lives, we can be sure there will always be enough. "I have been young, and now am old; yet have I not seen the righteous forsaken, nor his seed begging bread" (Psalms 37:25).

2) To meet the needs of others.

A second reason God gives us money is so we can meet the needs of others. This was illustrated beautifully on the day of Pentecost. Those early believers, were so filled with the Spirit of God, and so in tune with God's will that many "sold their possessions and goods, and parted them to all men, as every man had need" (Acts 2:45). In this case, many had traveled a great distance to participate in the feast—and had not made arrangements to stay for a longer period of time. After the Holy Spirit was poured out, these new believers felt a strong need to stay in Jerusalem, and get more training in the principles of the Gospel. Those with resources shared them freely to help make that possible.

Paul encouraged this kind of sharing as well: "Distribute to the necessity of saints" (Romans 12:13) he wrote in one place. In another he urged them: "your abundance may be a supply for their want, that their abundance also may be a supply for your want" (II Corinthians 8:14). When that happens, he added, it will be like gathering manna in the days of Moses: "he that had gathered much had nothing over; and he that had gathered little had no lack" (II Corinthians 8:15). There is ample wealth in this world. If those with more gave more generously to those with less, there would be plenty for all.

Remembering that God gives us resources so we can meet the needs of others is an important principle. And it is supposed to influence how we use our money.

3) To provide guidance.

Here's a final way I believe God uses money—to provide guidance. Consider for example the story of Elijah. After pronouncing a drought on Israel, God instructed the prophet to flee to the brook Cherith, and hide himself, adding "I have commanded the ravens to feed thee there" (I Kings 17:4). And every day, "the ravens brought him bread and flesh in the morning, and bread and flesh in the evening; and he drank of the brook" (I Kings 17:6).

But in the course of time, the brook dried up (I Kings 17:7), and presumably the ravens stopped coming. This signaled that it was time for a change in direction for Elijah. God could have kept His provision flowing to Elijah there, but He had something different in mind. He was to go to Zarephath and stay with a certain widow there, where God's support would be just as supernatural. In other words, God used provision (or the lack thereof), to communicate direction.

In my experience, I have seen God's miraculous provision many times. Often ministry commitments, left us tight on income, and yet time and again, we would see God provide for our needs. Sometimes an unexpected expense would come up, and a gift would come in at just the right time—that matched that exact cost. In fact, looking back—I can't help but see generally that God always expanded or diminished our income to match our needs in ways that defy rational explanation. These miracles were always a strong affirmation that we were on the right path.

At other times, I would have some crazy idea for some big project, but the funds would simply not materialize. I took this as an indication that my idea wasn't quite right, or that it wasn't the right time. After all, the promise in II Corinthians 9:8 was that "God is able to make all grace abound toward you; that ye always having all sufficiency in all things, may abound to every good work". Given the astonishing comprehensiveness of that verse (all grace, always, all sufficiency, all things, every work, etc.), it seemed clear to me God's work done in God's way, would never lack God's supply. I've learned to trust God's leading through finances.

So these are the three purposes for money that I see in Scripture. To meet our own needs. To meet the needs of others. And to give direction to our life.

In the coming days, we are going to look at the implications of these concepts in our money management decisions. Stay tuned...

Foundational Principles
Study Questions

Take a moment to summarize what money is, and what makes it so valuable:

What are God's three purposes for money? Include a reference or two for each.

How important is it to understand God's purposes for money? And more, to use our money in ways that are in harmony with His purposes?

Additional Notes:

Get a Grip
Chapter 3

So far we have seen that God wants to bless us financially. Not primarily so we can gather up a huge pile of cash, but rather, so we will always have the resources required to meet our needs. And to meet the needs of others. God also uses money to communicate direction to our life.

Now it's time to start getting into the nitty gritty of things. How do we actually manage our money in such a way as to ensure it is accomplishing God's intended purposes? Or to put it differently, how do we get a grip?

Counting the Cost

Jesus highlighted the key to this, while preaching to the crowds one day. "For which of you, intending to build a tower, sitteth not down first, and counteth the cost, whether he have sufficient to finish it?" (Luke 14:28). Clearly, when attempting to do something, it is important to carefully consider what costs are involved, and the resources you have available to meet those costs. Otherwise, if a person runs short, and is not able to finish it, "all that behold it begin to mock him, saying, this man began to build, and was not able to finish" (Luke 14:29-30). No one wants that!

In terms of money management, this process of counting the cost (expenses), and determining whether or not you have enough to cover them (income) is called budgeting. Or more specifically, a budget allows us to intentionally allocate our resources to various categories in such a way that we make sure all our bills get paid!

To get a grip, we just need to devise a plan that limits our expenses to our income.

How to Budget

There are many software programs available for this kind of thing, but it doesn't have to be complicated. Line up all your non-negotiable expenses (bills), and subtract that from your total income each month. Set that amount aside. Then take what is left over, and allocate it to several discretionary accounts as the Lord leads: eating out, new clothes, hobbies, gifts, savings, whatever. Prayerfully and thoughtfully, create an ideal plan for how you would most like to spend that money, and stick to it.

If you struggle with self-discipline, try this: every payday, put the specified amount of cash in separate envelopes for each of those discretionary allocations—and then spend exclusively out of those envelopes. (Keep the rest in your checking account for your bills). When an envelope is empty, you simply stop spending in that area, until more money comes in. Don't take from other categories. And don't borrow against the future.

Stick to your plan. And tweak as needed each month. That's all there is to it.

If you anticipate your income and expenses correctly each month, you should always have enough to make it through to your next payday. To get one more section of that tower built.

Making Ends Meet

If after careful analysis, you realize your expenses exceed your income, you have a problem. And there are only a limited number of solutions. You can either 1) increase your income, or 2) decrease your expenses.

Sometimes we can increase the income side of the equation. Maybe we can find a higher paying job, a second part-time job, or some kind of personal side hustle. Moses urged the children of Israel to remember it was God "that giveth thee power to get wealth" (Deuteronomy 8:18), and He still does that today. He can inspire us with all sorts of creative ideas to generate a little extra money consistently.

But usually it's faster and easier to decrease expenses. According to Paul, "godliness with contentment is great gain. For we brought nothing into this world, and it is certain we can carry nothing out. And having food and raiment let us be therewith content" (I Timothy 6:6-8). In our modern materialistic world, we're constantly being influenced (manipulated) to want all sorts of things that go far beyond this biblical minimum of food and clothes. Looking for ways to cut back on anything that exceeds this short list, will suggest many ways to reduce expenses.

Don't minimize the importance of small things. Jesus emphasized this point explicitly: "He that is faithful in that which is least is faithful also in much: and he that is unjust in the least is unjust also in much" (Luke 16:10). And in fact, He was talking specifically about money here, for He added "if therefore you have not been faithful in the unrighteous mammon [money], who will commit to your trust the true riches" (Luke 16:11)? In other words, learning to be faithful in our smallest expenditures is a spiritual issue, with serious spiritual implications...

At the same time, don't overlook the big items in your budget. Sometimes moving into a smaller house, or keeping your car for an extra year or two can save hundreds of dollars a month. And that can go a long way toward making sure your income exceeds your expenses.

If you want to get a grip on your money, there's only one way to do it. Create a budget. Develop a plan that allocates your income to various expense categories, in a way that prayerfully harmonizes with God's three purposes for money as closely as possible. And then, stick to your plan.

Whatever it takes, whether by increasing income or decreasing expenses, you have to make ends meet. You must count the cost, and make sure you have sufficient to get through that month. You have to get a grip.

Proverbs 10:4
He becometh poor that dealeth with a slack hand:
but the hand of the diligent maketh rich.

Tomorrow we look at what happens when we fail to achieve this step.

Get a Grip
Study Questions

What can we learn from the story of the man building a tower that can help us with money management?

What is a budget? And how does it work?

What are the only two ways to get a budget to balance?

Why is it important to be faithful in small purchases? In large purchases?

How important is it to "get a grip" on our finances?

Additional Notes:

The Dangers of Debt
Chapter 4

So God wants to bless us financially. And the Bible suggests He does this for specific reasons—to meet our needs, so we can meet the needs of others, and to give direction and guidance. Our part is to manage our resources in harmony with those purposes. And to do that we use a budget to get a grip.

Today I want to identify one of the greatest dangers to money management: debt.

Owe No Man

Paul stated this principle quite clearly in the book of Romans: "Owe no man any thing, but to love one another" (Romans 13:8). The only debt we should accept willingly is the debt of compassion for others.

I'm not suggesting that it is a sin to borrow, or to be in debt. But I am suggesting it is an indicator we are doing something wrong. In that same chapter on blessings and cursings we looked at on Day 1, God makes it clear that when we fail to follow His counsels, strangers "shall lend to thee, and thou shalt not lend to him: he shall be the head, and thou shalt be the tail" (Deuteronomy 28:44). Contrariwise, when we do obey, "the LORD shall make thee the head, and not the tail; and thou shalt be above only, and thou shalt not be beneath" (Deuteronomy 28:13). We should never have to borrow.

It is similar to disease. Being sick is not a sin, but many times it is a symptom that we have failed to follow some health principle. In the same way, debt is generally an indicator we have violated some financial principle.

And given the debt levels of the average person, and even of whole countries, it seems pretty clear there is a lot of financial sickness going around!

True Freedom

As I've reflected on this topic over the years, I've been impressed with a number of biblical reasons for why we should avoid debt. Here's my short list:

1) First and foremost, it leaves us entangled. Paul reminds us that "no man that warreth entangleth himself with the affairs of this life; that he may please him who hath chosen him to be a soldier" (II Timothy 2:4). If a person is burdened with debt it becomes very difficult to respond to God's calls to ministry. I've seen many people over the years forced to refuse great service opportunities, because they had too many bills. They were entangled.

2) James points out another danger. He warns that many of us "ask amiss, that ye may consume it upon your lusts" (James 4:3). Sometimes God restricts our income to help ensure we don't spend it on "foolish and hurtful lusts, which drown men in destruction and perdition" (I Timothy 6:9). Borrowing is a way to bypass that protection, and indulge in our desires anyway. That is, it short-circuits God's third purpose for money—to give direction. Rather than trusting God's wisdom in not providing something, we finagle a way to purchase it anyway.

3) Borrowing also hinders our ability to follow God's second purpose for money—helping others. If we are so burdened by debt that much of our future income is already committed, it becomes very difficult to stop and give generously as God reveals needs to us. Paul urges us to "bear ye one another's burdens, and so fulfil the law of Christ" (Galatians 6:2). Debt makes that difficult. And we miss out on the return blessing: "Give and it shall be given unto you ... pressed down, and shaken together, and running over" (Luke 6:38). The more we give, the more God gives to us!

4). Another danger highlighted in the book of James is that of presuming upon the future. Specifically, he warns against those who make plans, saying "we will go into such a city, and continue there a year, and buy and sell, and get gain" (James 4:13), when the reality is, we "know not what shall be on the morrow" (James 4:14). Planning is important of course, but if our plans require us to take on debt, and then there is an unexpected downturn of some sort, we will find our self in a difficult situation. Bottom line: the future is unknowable (Proverbs 5:6). Don't gamble on it.

Compound Interest

In addition to these biblical reasons, it is simply poor money management. Most people don't really grasp how compound interest works. Compound interest refers to the way interest accumulates not just on the principal borrowed, but also on the interest amounts added to it. And then we pay interest on the interest on the interest, and so on.

Take for example credit card debt. Suppose you have a card with an interest rate of 18%, and you increase your balance every year by just $1000, for 10 years. Rather than owing $10,000 plus a little more, here's how it actually adds up:

Year	Borrow	Interest	Balance
1	$1000	$180	$1180
2	$1000	$392	$2572
3	$1000	$643	$4215
4	$1000	$939	$6154
5	$1000	$1288	$8441
6	$1000	$1700	$11141
7	$1000	$2185	$14326
8	$1000	$2758	$18085
9	$1000	$3435	$22521
10	$1000	$4234	$27755

You end up owing nearly three times the amount you borrowed!

Worse, the interest continues to compound on that full balance while you attempt to pay this down! In fact, if you paid back $1000 a year for the next ten years, you would actually end up with more than $100,000 in debt! Incredible.

To successfully pay this down in the next ten years, your annual payment needs to actually be well over $5000 per year:

Year	Payment	Interest	Balance
1	$5234	$4054	$26575
2	$5234	$3841	$25182
3	$5234	$3591	$23539
4	$5234	$3295	$21600
5	$5234	$2946	$19312
6	$5234	$2534	$16611
7	$5234	$2048	$13426
8	$5234	$1475	$9666
9	$5234	$798	$5230
10	$5230	$0	$0

Essentially, for every little $1000 indulgence you put on your card, because you didn't have the funds on hand—it didn't cost you $1000—but $5234 dollars! Think about that the next time you pull out your credit card!

Or to look at it differently, the interest on your relatively small $10,000 dollar "loan" came to over $42,000 dollars over the course of twenty years. Actually, it would probably be even more, because this illustration only compounds the interest once a year, rather than continuously like most credit card companies do.

Now I don't want to go into a rant on this, but I personally believe most of the inequality in this world can be directly traced to this financial reality. Those who borrow are essentially pouring their money, year after year, into the hands of those who lend to them.

And for Christians to do this, it is simply poor stewardship.

Don't Co-Sign

On another related, but important side note: don't co-sign for someone else's debt either. The Bible calls that "surety" and suggests it is even worse than borrowing. "My son, if thou be surety for thy friend ... thou are snared with the words of the mouth. Do this now, my son, and deliver thyself" (Proverbs 6:1-3).

What makes it so bad? Here's the obvious reason: if they default—you get stuck with the bill, but don't even get the item that was purchased!

Seriously, if a bank won't lend to someone, it's usually because there is a reason. Give your friend money if you want, but don't put your good name at jeopardy! "A good name is better than precious ointment" (Ecclesiastes 7:1).

In conclusion, avoid debt wherever possible. It keeps you from responding freely to the call of God. And it's just poor money management. If you are in debt, come up with a plan to get out, and stay out.

Here's how one writer put it over a hundred years ago: "Deny yourself a thousand things rather than run in debt. This has been the curse of your life, getting into debt. Avoid it as you would the smallpox" (Counsels on Stewardship, p 230). And we all know about plagues, these days, don't we?

Tomorrow we will look at the secret to never having to borrow.

The Dangers of Debt
Study Questions

What is the only debt believers should willingly accept?

What is debt a symptom of?

What are four reasons we should avoid debt

Explain how compound interest dramatically increases the cost of purchases.

What does the Bible say about co-signing for someone?

We should avoid debt like what?

Additional Notes:

Treasure in the House
Chapter 5

Yesterday's topic may have sparked some questions in your mind. Is it ever right to borrow? What about for a car or for a house? What about borrowing to grow your business? Or to build a church?

Today I want to suggest that's not really the right question. The better question may be, does God have a better plan? And I believe the answer to that question is yes.

Treasure for the Wise

The book of Proverbs clearly teaches that saving money is a wise thing to do. "There is treasure to be desired and oil in the dwelling of the wise; but a foolish man spendeth it up" (Proverbs 21:20). If your budget does not include some amount to be set aside each month for savings, then you are going to have a problem whenever there is an unexpected expense. You'll either have to borrow from some other category, or borrow against the future (debt). But with savings, you can cover those surprise expenses.

In fact, a wise person is going to have a lot of savings. "In the house of the righteous is much treasure: but in the revenues of the wicked is trouble" (Proverbs 15:6). That last part of this verse reminds us that it doesn't matter how much we have coming in, if our expenses exceed our income, there is always going to be trouble. But the opposite is also true, even if we only have a modest income—if we manage to save a bit every month, our pile is going to grow and grow and grow. That's the goal.

Most financial experts recommend saving at least 10% of our income every month. If you can't start at that level, do whatever percent you can, and then divert at least half of every raise you get toward savings until you are at this level or more. And when it comes to savings, the sooner you start, the better!

Consider the Ants

Proverbs encourages us to learn the importance of saving for the future from the ants. These tiny creatures work hard during the summer, storing food for the winter—so when tough times come, they are fully prepared.

> *Proverbs 6:6-8*
> *Go to the ant, thou sluggard; consider her ways, and be wise: Which having no guide, overseer, or ruler, provideth her meat in the summer, and gathereth her food in the harvest.*

There's at least a couple lessons we can learn from this. First, when times are prosperous, we should avoid splurging. Food is plentiful for ants during the harvest season—but that is the time to save as much of that excess as possible. It's not time to eat as much as we can! So whenever you get that big bonus at work, or maybe a tax refund, or some other windfall—that's not the time to buy something extravagant. Stick as much of that extra money as possible into your savings account.

Second, this passage highlights the importance of thinking ahead. One of the biggest challenges people have with sticking to a budget, is they forget infrequent large expenses. Let's say you have a car insurance payment, twice every year at $600. It's easy to overlook that in your monthly budget—and when the bill comes due we can't pay it. What we should be doing is setting aside $100 every month for this expense—so when the due date rolls around we have those funds on hand. The same is true for property taxes and other annual payments. Where I live, I can get a big discount on heating costs if I pay for my winter fuel up front. So I prepare for that payment, which comes in July—it's a sizeable amount where I live, but it saves me hundreds of dollars every year.

There are countless other benefits to having some savings in the bank. It enables you to take advantage of special opportunities that come up. Or to buy things in bulk at a discount. Or to take advantage of a big sale. But the best is just some peace of mind—knowing you have reserves on hand if needed. Having a little nest egg is priceless.

And ultimately, saving is the key to never having to borrow.

Common Questions

But what about big expenses, like a car or a house? Is there ever a time to borrow? What do we do if we can't wait to buy something, and there is a real need? What if there's no time to save money for a needed big purchase?

It's true, we do need shelter and transportation. And if we don't have savings, we may have to finance those purchases. But that is usually an indication that we have not been saving properly all along.

Let's take the purchase of a car. Depending on where we live, having a vehicle can definitely be a legitimate need. And many of us don't have cash on hand to go out and buy that shiny new model that catches our attention. My recommendation in that case, is to buy instead the least expensive car you can, and borrow as little as possible for it. Then, start saving immediately for the next car, as if you were making a car payment for that nice car you actually wanted.

When it is finally time to trade your car in, spend no more than what you have in that specific savings category. And then continue saving money for the next car. After a few rounds of this, you will have plenty of money to pay cash for something you really want.

In the long run, you will pay less. You will be collecting interest on your savings, and not paying interest to some auto lender. You are making compound interest work for you!

What about buying a house? Isn't that a good investment? And who has money to pay cash for a house? Houses do tend to appreciate in value—and it's almost always better to buy than to rent, as at least part of your mortgage payment goes to paying off the principle. So my advice is to own a house if you can.

But again, start with the least expensive house possible, and pay down that debt as fast as possible—paying as much each month as you would have paid for that nicer house you wanted! That will enable you to quickly build up some equity in the house, which you can use to make a bigger down payment on your next home—thus keeping your payments (interest) low. Keep doubling up on those payments though as if you were in an even nicer home and then in time leap frog up to your next house.

Experts who recommend this approach say you can get the house you want paid for in about half the time (half the money) as it would have taken to buy the more expensive house outright. Why? All that extra money goes to pay huge amounts of interest. Or to put differently, if you build up slowly, you can live in that nicer house for free after 15 years, instead of after 30.

We took out a mortgage when we bought our first house—and were very fortunate. We bought when the market was low. Paid extra every month. And sold when the market was high. And we made enough equity in those seven years to pay cash for our next house. No more mortgage payments for us!

What about borrowing to build your business, or build a church? There may be situations where this can be of benefit to you. And the urgency of the times we live in may even demand it on occasion. But the Bible gives a powerful story about what I believe is God's preferred method.

It's the story of King David. His desire was to build a temple for God. But because of all the violence in his life, God said no. That task would fall to his son Solomon. So David, instead, spent the rest of his life saving and preparing for that building. Specifically, "I have prepared for the house of the LORD an hundred thousand talents of gold, and a thousand thousand talents of silver; and of brass and iron without weight; for it is in abundance: timber also and stone have I prepared" (I Chronicles 22:14).

Those years of saving enabled him to amass an incredible amount of treasure—which Solomon then used to build a temple far more glorious and magnificent than anything David might have originally conceived. It led to a building that was one of the wonders of the world. And all without debt.

There is power in savings. It smooths out all sorts of bumps in the road. It brings stability and security to our lives. And it makes big things possible.

We don't need to save massive amounts—but having reserves on hand will help every dollar we do have go further. It's a part of God's financial plan for every believer!

Tomorrow we look at how to accumulate wealth even faster...

Treasure in the House
Study Questions

What does the Bible say a wise person will save up in his house? How much?

How much do experts recommend saving?

What are two lessons we can learn from ants?

Explain how to minimize debt when it comes to big purchases, like a car or house?

How did God finance the building of the first temple?

Additional Notes:

With All Thy Might
Chapter 6

So far we've looked at a number of critical principles in money management. Particularly: God's purposes for money, the importance of budgeting, avoiding debt, and the need for savings. These principles will carry you a long way toward financial success.

But there is another key principle I want to look at today, that has the potential to unlock all sorts of prosperity in your life. And it's a principle not usually discussed in most money management training.

Why? Because it has to do with character.

Giving our Best

Here's how the book of Ecclesiastes words this principle: "whatsoever thy hand findeth to do, do it with thy might; for there is no work, nor device, nor knowledge, nor wisdom, in the grave, whither thou goest" (Ecclesiastes 9:10). Life is short. Our time here is limited. So whatever we set out to do, we need to approach it wholeheartedly. To put our very best into it.

Paul wrote something similar: "Whatsoever ye do, do it heartily, as to the Lord, and not unto men; knowing that of the Lord ye shall receive the reward of the inheritance: for ye serve the Lord Christ" (Colossians 3:23-24). The literal translation of "heartily" means "from the soul". Paul is saying we need to fully engage all our mental powers towards our tasks. Again, it's about giving every task our best.

And in this case, not just because our time on earth is short. It's also because what we're doing is spiritual. We serve the Lord Christ. And there is a reward for those who do so "heartily"!

The Life of Diligence

Proverbs calls this kind of life, a life of diligence. And it promises many financial blessings to those who cultivate this sort of character. "The hand of the diligent maketh rich" (Proverbs 10:4). "The hand of the diligent shall bear rule" (Proverbs 12:24). "The soul of the diligent shall be made fat" (Proverbs 13:4). "The thoughts of the diligent tend only to plenteousness" (Proverbs 12:5). "Seest thou a man diligent in his business? He shall stand before kings" (Proverbs 22:29). And so on.

Diligence is the path to prosperity and success.

The problem is we don't often really know what a life of diligence looks like. I've been fascinated by this particular word for a long time and spent years pouring over the book of Proverbs to try and glean insights into what it means. And what I've discovered is that it is a multi-faceted gemstone. That is, diligence consists of a mixture of different qualities.

While I can only scratch the surface of what the Bible has to say about diligence here, allow me to highlight at least a few of its chief characteristics:

1) A diligent person works hard, without supervision. Proverbs 6:6-8.

2) A diligent person doesn't procrastinate. Proverbs 20:4.

3) A diligent person doesn't use excuses to avoid action. Proverbs 22:13.

4) A diligent person pays attention to small details. Proverbs 24:30-32.

5) A diligent person researches key information. Proverbs 27:23-24.

6) A diligent person refuses to sleep in. Proverbs 26:14.

7) A diligent person finishes the projects he starts. Proverbs 12:27.

You could reflect on those same verses and draw out even more principles if you wanted. Foresight. Self-denial. Planning. Attentiveness. Preparation. Thoroughness. Responsibility. Industry. And so on. The Bible, basically, is painting a picture of an individual that is thoroughly well-rounded. They have learned how to think and to do. And to do things well!

In other words, a diligent person makes stuff happen.

Most of us have strong and weak spots when it comes to diligence. I've always been full of ideas, and eager to start new projects—but I had to learn how to be a finisher, and follow those projects through to their conclusion. I didn't have trouble working hard without supervision, but I still struggle sometimes to get up as early as I'd like. And you too, probably have more of some aspects of diligence in your character, and less of others. But good money management involves cultivating as many of these qualities as possible...

A Simple Example

Let me share a simple example of how diligence works. Suppose you were to listen to a sermon, and hear for the first time, the importance of memorizing Scripture. And you go home inspired to give it a try. If you are diligent, you are going to get started right away. (No procrastination!) Maybe you'll ask around and do some research on how to memorize. You develop a plan. You work hard at it, giving it your best. If things don't go well at first, you do more research, read a book or take a class—until you figure out the problem and you tweak your strategy. And no matter what, you refuse to get discouraged. Or to make excuses. Ultimately, because you work at it consistently, and persevere with it over time, you soon accumulate dozens, or even hundreds of verses. One day maybe, if you remain diligent, you'll have a thousand verses! And more...

But that's not usually how it happens, is it? Most people go home, inspired perhaps, but they put off getting started. Or if they do decide to give it a try, they don't do any research, or put much thought into developing a plan. And they only put half-hearted efforts into actually memorizing. And if things don't go well right from the start, they quickly get discouraged. They start making excuses for why they can't memorize. They become hit or miss in the efforts. And before long they've given up completely—and any verses they learned early on slip away forever! Doesn't this story sound familiar?

To put it bluntly, diligence makes the entire difference between success and failure. And this same rule applies to every aspect of discipleship. In fact, it applies to every aspect of life.

When you apply a diligent mindset at your job, you will tackle every challenge with excellence. You'll solve problems, work out obstacles, teach yourself important skills, and generally get things done. And your employer will notice, leading to raises, and faster promotions.

You're also constantly working to acquire skills outside of work. You learn to do all sorts of things. Repair things. Make things. Maybe you invest some of your savings in useful tools—to enable you to do even more. Soon other people are asking for your services. These skills not only save you a lot of money, they may end up generating extra income too.

And because you tackle these side projects just as diligently—they may actually take off. Perhaps swelling into their own small businesses. In fact, one day, you may go transition to working for yourself full time. Or even have employees working for you!

And the more you keep learning and growing and working, the more your revenue just keeps climbing higher. It's just a matter of time. Diligence inevitably leads to prosperity!

If you really want to be successful in life, aim for diligence. Learn to be a doer, someone that makes things happen. And God will give you all the ideas you need to get ahead.

"Remember, the LORD thy God: for it is he that giveth thee power to get wealth" (Deuteronomy 8:18). If we put our hand and heart to whatever lies before us, we'll see God opening doors for our blessing.

Try it, diligence works.

With All Thy Might
Study Questions

How does the Bible say we should tackle the tasks before us?

What does God say will happen to those who are diligent?

List the 7 characteristics of diligence suggested in the lesson. Jot down additional qualities if you like:

In which of these areas are you strong? And in which are you weak?

Give an example of how diligence can lead to success.

How can diligence lead to financial success?

Additional Notes:

Heaven's Mathematics
Chapter 7

We're drawing near the end of our course, and we've covered a lot already. First and foremost, God's purposes for money. But also budgeting, debt, savings, and diligence. Today we are going to look at another key principle. Two actually.

I call this section, heaven's mathematics...

Heaven's Storehouse

The Bible gives explicit instructions in a number of places, that God expects us to return a portion of our income to Him. That amount, (10%), is called the tithe. And God promises a blessing to us if we comply with these instructions:

> *Malachi 3:10*
> *Bring ye all the tithes into the storehouse, that there may be meat in mine house, and prove me now herewith, saith the LORD of hosts, if I will not open you the windows of heaven, and pour you out a blessing, that there shall not be room enough to receive it.*

The passage goes on to say that God will rebuke the devourer for our sakes—ensuring our gardens and fields are fruitful. In fact, our blessings will be so obvious, the nations around us will take notice of it, and call us blessed!

Note that this tithe is supposed to be the first part of our income not the last. To quote Proverbs: "Honour the LORD with thy substance, and with the firstfruits of all thine increase" (Proverbs 3:9). And the result? Once again, "thy barns be filled with plenty, and thy presses shall burst out with new wine" (Proverbs 3:10).

Granted, it doesn't make sense from a human perspective how giving away 10% of our income will somehow make the remaining 90% stretch even further. But I'm convinced it's true. And there are countless thousands of believers around the world who will eagerly testify to this fact as well. My wife and I have done this for years, and we have never been disappointed by God's provision for us.

The Bible certainly teaches a failure to do this can have an adverse effect on finances. In the book of Haggai, God's people were not giving to God as expected, and the results were pretty serious. "Ye have sown much, and bring in little; ye eat, but ye have not enough; ye drink, but ye are not filled with drink; ye clothe you, but there is none warm; and he that earneth wages earneth wages to put it into a bag with holes" (Haggai 1:6). That's quite a picture isn't it? Putting your money into a bag with holes?

It's pretty clear, God was interfering with things so no matter what they tried, it just never seemed to work like it was supposed to. "Ye looked for much" God says, but "when ye brought it home, I did blow upon it" (Haggai 1:9). In this case, it had to do with their apathy in rebuilding the temple. But the same is surely true for those who withhold their tithes from God: "Ye are cursed with a curse: for ye have robbed me, even this whole nation" (Malachi 3:9). "Wherein have we robbed thee?" they asked. "In tithes and offerings" (Malachi 3:8) God answered.

If you think the best time to start tithing is when your finances are caught up, think again. That may be the actual reason your finances are running behind.

Personally, I believe tithing is a test of **faithfulness**. God gave specific instructions on how much to return, where to return it (the storehouse), and what it was to be used for (the support of the Levites). The test here, is over our willingness to follow these instructions. In essence, it is a test to see which has first priority in our life: God or money.

And if He has first place, He can trust us with more.

Freewill Offerings

That last verse suggested there are actually two ways to rob God. One is withholding our tithes. The other is withholding freewill offerings. In the latter case, God does not specify the amount, where to give it, or what it should be used for. That's all entirely up to our discretion.

But the promised blessing is just as abundant. "Give, and it shall be given unto you; good measure, pressed down, and shaken together, and running over, shall men give into your bosom" (Luke 6:38). It's kind of like the blessing promised to those who tithe. The return blessing will be so great "there shall not be room to receive it" (Malachi 3:10). I'm not suggesting we give to get more back—only that if you give generously, it will actually strengthen your finances! Or as the old saying goes, you can't out give God.

The rest of that verse in Luke actually continues with that correlation: "for with the same measure that ye mete withal it shall be measured to you again". It's wholly inexplicable. God is promising in this case to reward us proportionally to how much we give.

Here's how Proverbs describes this principle: "The liberal soul shall be made fat: and he that watereth shall be watered also himself" (Proverbs 11:25). And the previous verse describes the opposite side of this. When a person "withholdeth more than is meet" the result is that "it tendeth to poverty" (Proverbs 11:24).

God is being pretty explicit here. He is saying the way we give—whether liberally or stingily—is going to have an impact on our own prosperity. Which clearly makes giving a financial principle too!

Paul expressed this same principle in these words: "He which soweth sparingly shall reap also sparingly; and he which soweth bountifully shall reap also bountifully" (II Corinthians 9:6). But he also reemphasizes the freedom each person has to chose regarding how they give. Every person "as he purposeth in his heart, so let him give; not grudgingly, or of necessity: for God loveth a cheerful giver" (II Corinthians 9:7). And then the reward if we do give freely: "God is able to make all grace abound toward you; that ye, always having all sufficiency in all things, may about to every good work" (II Corinthians 9:8). We've looked at that verse before—it's pretty massively comprehensive!

From my study of these verses it seems pretty clear that offerings are a different kind of test. While tithing is a test of faithfulness, offerings are a test of **generosity**. When we give willingly, and bountifully, and cheerfully, it shows God that money does not have a stranglehold on our soul. And He's greatly pleased by that.

And once again, that means He can trust us with more.

So this is how heaven's mathematics works. If you are faithful to return our tithes to God, in the amount, at the location, and for the purpose He has specified—the remaining amount will magically expand to make up for the rest.

And if we go on to generously give beyond that amount, to other causes and needs, however God leads us to give—He will expand whatever is left over even more. In fact, the more we give, the more He will bless.

These are the two tests. Tithes and offerings. One is a test of faithfulness, the other a test of generosity. Implement both these principles in your money management, and you can look forward to seeing what God does...

Heaven's Mathematics
Study Questions

Summarize what the Bible teaches about tithing.

List some of the things specified about the tithe?

How will tithing affect our finances? What about a failure to tithe?

Explain how tithing is a test of *faithfulness*:

What does God promise to those who give freewill offerings as well?

Why do you think the blessing for these is proportional to our giving?

How are offerings a test of *generosity*?

Additional Notes:

The Love of Money
Chapter 8

We've come to the final study in this short class on money management. And we've got a doozy of a topic. While our previous studies have all zoomed in on how God wants to bless us, and how we can cooperate with Him in receiving that blessing, this one takes a slightly more sobering approach.

In particular we are going to look briefly at some of the Bible's many warnings about money. And particularly how dangerous, the love of money can be...

The Love of Money
The Bible certainly gives some stern warnings on this topic, and we can't close this class without looking at some of these verses. Paul, for example, wrote one of his harshest warning anywhere in the Bible on the love of money. Here's the verse:

> *I Timothy 6:10-11*
> *10 For the love of money is the root of all evil: which while some coveted after, they have erred from the faith, and pierced themselves through with many sorrows. 11 But thou, O man of God, flee these*

things; and follow after righteousness, godliness, faith, love, patience, meekness.

Now it's clear Paul is talking about the love of money, not money itself. And his counsel to flee these things is not advice to run from money, but to avoid coveting, erring from the faith, piercing our self through with sorrows.

Still, this warning is pretty sobering, isn't it? Because money is so incredibly valuable, the temptation is always going to be there, to get emotionally attached to it. And that is what Paul is warning us about.

There are several ways money can trouble us. In verse 9 of this same chapter, Paul says "they that will be rich fall into temptation and a snare, and into many foolish and hurtful lusts, which drown men in destruction and perdition" (I Timothy 6:9). The drive to achieve success can leave us tempted to compromise our values—and thus put our soul in serious danger.

And if we manage to succeed in becoming rich, there are even more dangers. Paul warns us a few verses later to "be not highminded, nor trust in uncertain riches, but in the living God, who giveth us richly all things to enjoy" (I Timothy 6:17). Wealth can spark pride, arrogance, and self-sufficiency—and all of these are spiritually deadly too.

A Cloud of Witnesses

The Bible is full of stories of individuals who were afflicted with this love of money. You can't help but skim through these stories and see how dangerous this temptation really is. Consider for example the following:

Achan

    This fellow saw some things he liked in Jericho and took and hid them for himself—even though they had been expressly consecrated to God. In the end, God exposed this sin, and it cost Achan his life, and the life of his family.

Balaam

    He was a prophet of God who was offered extensive bribes to curse Israel. Though God warned him against doing that—he went anyway, and figured out a way to cause Israel grave problems. He ended up getting killed in a battle between the Jews and the Midianites.

Gehazi

    This man, who was Elisha's servant, decided to take advantage of Elisha healing Naaman to get some rewards for himself. He ended up getting Naaman's leprosy instead.

The Rich Young Ruler

    This man came to Jesus seeking eternal life, but apparently his riches were more important to him. And he went away sorrowful, unwilling to pay the cost of following Jesus.

Judas Iscariot

    This man was one of the most promising of the disciples of Jesus. But he had a hidden weak spot—he was a thief. And he ended up betraying Jesus, tragically, for 30 pieces of silver.

Ananias and Sapphira

    These two sold some land and donated it to the early church—but they secretly kept back part of it for themselves. Worse, they lied about it. Both were struck down dead, one after the other.

Demas

This man was a co-laborer with Paul, and was mentioned by him positively in at least two of his epistles. But he later ended up abandoning Paul, having loved this present world a bit too much.

I'm sure you can think of other examples. All of these stories illustrate just how dangerous, and ultimately how devastating, the love of money can be. Every believer must determine to fight against it.

An Evil Eye

Jesus Himself highlighted the dangers inherent in the pursuit of wealth. And He makes the point—that the problem is our focus. In the Sermon on the Mount, Jesus urged us to "lay not up for yourselves treasures upon earth," because this world is transitory, fleeting, fickle. And instead to "lay up for yourselves treasures in heaven," because that world is eternal, unchanging, sure. And then this bombshell verse:

> *Matthew 6:21*
> *For where your treasure is, there will your heart be also.*

Notice it doesn't say you put your treasure where your heart is. It says, wherever you put your treasure—there your heart will follow. If our focus is temporal wealth, we'll be caught up with the things of this world. If our focus is the kingdom of God, we'll be caught up with the things of heaven. It's an inescapable law of the mind.

Over the next couple verses, Jesus zooms in again on the importance of focus. "The light of the body is the eye: if therefore thine eye be single, thy whole body shall be full of light" (Matthew 6:22). That's the goal—a single focus. To be so single-minded our life is filled to the brim with God's Spirit!

"But," Jesus continues, "if thine eye be evil, thy whole body shall be full of darkness" (Matthew 6:23). What is that evil eye? Given the context, it's almost certain He was alluding to Proverbs 28:22, which says "he that hasteth to be rich hath an evil eye." To put our focus on wealth is to fill our soul with darkness.

And as if to make sure there was no question about what He was saying, Jesus threw in one more verse: "No man can serve two masters ... Ye cannot serve God and [money]" (Matthew 6:24). It's one or the other.

In closing our study of financial principles, let's settle in on one issue—God must always remain first priority. We must fully commit to following His principles. To acquiring money in the way He stipulates, and to using that money according to His purposes too.

God wants to bless us financially, the Bible is clear on that. But we must enter into that pursuit in full cooperation with God. Fully submitted to Him, and His will.

May the Lord bless you, in your finances. Money matters.

The Love of Money
Study Questions

What does the Bible have to say about the love of money? What makes it so dangerous?

Give examples of Bible characters who gave in to this temptation. What were the consequences of this in their lives?

What does Jesus say about how treasure affects our heart?

How important is it to keep God at the center of our focus?

Additional Notes:

FAST Missions
Cutting-Edge Tools and Training

Ready to become a Revival Agent? FAST Missions can help! Our comprehensive training curriculum will give you the skills you need to take in God's Word effectively, live it out practically, and pass it on to others consistently.

Eager to start memorizing God's Word? Our powerful keys will transform your ability to hide Scripture in your heart.

Want to explore the secrets of "real life" discipleship? Our next level training zooms in on critical keys to growth, like Bible study, prayer, time management, and more.

Want to become a worker in the cause of Christ? Our most advanced training is designed to give you the exact ministry skills you need to see revival spread.

For more information, please visit us at:
WWW.FASTMISSIONS.COM

Study Guides

Looking for life-changing study guides to use in your small group or Bible study class? These resources have been used by thousands around the world. You could be next!

Survival Kit
Want to learn how to memorize Scripture effectively? These study guides will teach you 10 keys to memorization, all drawn straight from the Bible. Our most popular course ever!

Basic Training
Discover nuts and bolts keys to the core skills of discipleship: prayer, Bible study, time management, and more. Then learn how to share these skills with others. It is the course that launched our ministry!

Revival Keys
Now as never before, God's people need revival. And these guides can show you how to spark revival in your family, church, and community. A great revival is coming. Are you ready?

Online Classes

Want to try out some of the resources available at FAST? Here is just a small sampling of courses from among dozens of personal and small group study resources:

Crash Course
Discover Bible-based keys to effective memorization.
http://fast.st/cc

Fact or Fiction
Does the Bible really predict future events? You be the judge.
http://fast.st/prophecy

Monkey Business
Find out how evolution flunks the science test.
http://fast.st/monkey

Revive
Want more of God's Spirit? Learn how to pursue revival.
http://fast.st/revive

The Lost Art
Rediscover New Testament keys to making disciples.
http://fast.st/lostart

Digital Tools

FAST offers a number of powerful "apps for the soul" you can use to grow in your walk with God. And many of these are completely free to anyone with an account. Some of these include:

Review Engine
Our powerful review engine is designed to help ensure effective longterm Bible memorization. Give it a try, it works!

Bible Reading
An innovative Bible reading tool to help you read through the entire Bible, at your own pace, and in any order you want.

Prayer Journal
Use this tool to organize important requests, and we'll remind you to pray for them on the schedule you want.

Time Management
Learn how to be more productive, by keeping track of what you need to do and when. Just log in daily and get stuff done.

For more information about more than twenty tools like these, please visit us at *http://fast.st/tools*.

Books

If the content of this little book stirred your heart, look for these titles by the same author.

For Such A Time...
A challenging look at the importance of memorization for the last days, including topics such as the Three Angel's messages and the Latter Rain.

Moral Machinery
Discover how our spiritual, mental, and physical faculties work together using the sanctuary as a blueprint. Astonishing insights that could revolutionize your life!

The Movement
Discover God's plan to finish the work through a powerful endtime movement. Gain critical insights into what lies just ahead for the remnant!

www.ingramcontent.com/pod-product-compliance
Lightning Source LLC
Chambersburg PA
CBHW060427050426
42449CB00009B/2179